Baby Birds Grow Up

CONTENTS

 NATIONAL GEOGRAPHIC  Hampton-Brown

School Publishing

Words with Long i

i_e

Look at each picture. Read the words.

Example:

d**im**e

b**it**e

f**iv**e

sl**id**e

b**ik**e

k**it**e

Key Words

Read the sentences. Match each sentence to one of the pictures.

Pink Birds

1. This **kind** of bird has pink legs.
2. A mother bird watches **over** chicks.
3. The mother bird **was** **almost** white when she **was** a chick.
4. **Both** the mother and the chick stand on one leg, not **two** .

The bird has a little pink. It is almost white.

Phonics Games

NGReach.com

3

Flamingos

by Kate Baker

What kind of bird is this?

It's a flamingo.

nest

A mother flamingo has an egg
in a mud nest. The mother will watch
over the egg almost all of the time.

chick

When it's time, a soft, white
chick will hatch.

The chick can flap its wings. But
it can't fly yet. It needs time to grow.

The mother keeps the chick
safe. One day, the chick will
grow up.

Then it will have pink on its body
like its mother. They will both have
two long legs.

Look! It can stand on just one leg.
It's such a fine flamingo! ❖

Words with Long i

Read these words.

dive	hide	fix	chick
shine	five	dine	glide

Find the words with long **i**.
Use letters to build them.

d i v e

Talk Together

Choose words from the box above to tell a partner about these birds.

Flamingos can _dive_ in the lake.

Endings -ed, -ing

Read the words. See how they change when you add endings.

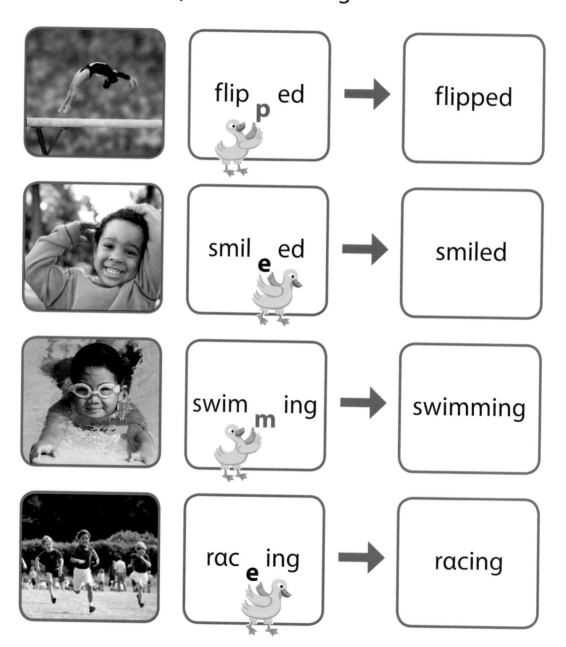

flip _p ed → flipped

smil _e ed → smiled

swim _m ing → swimming

rac _e ing → racing

High Frequency Words

almost
both
kind
over
two
was

Key Words

Look at the pictures.
Read the sentences.

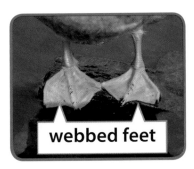
webbed feet

Ducks

1. This **kind** of bird has webbed feet.
2. The mother duck **was** watching **over** the little ducks.
3. **Both** ducks are **almost** at the lake.
4. The **two** ducks are swimming in the lake.

Almost all birds can fly.

GO! **Phonics Games**
NGReach.com

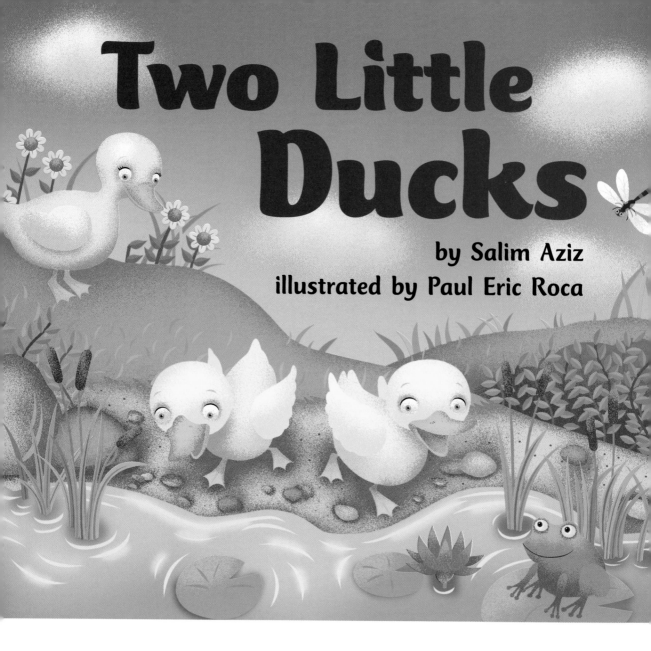

Two Little Ducks

by Salim Aziz

illustrated by Paul Eric Roca

It was time for a swim. Two
ducks ran over the hill. Quack,
quack, quack!

Little feet slap, slap, slapped.

Little wings flap, flap, flapped.

They jumped in the lake.

The ducks bobbed around. They flapped their feet. A duck needs both feet for swimming.

They looked for a fish to catch.

A fish swam by. One duck tipped his

body in.

Swish! His tail flipped up. He
got all wet. He trapped the fish.

The little ducks flapped in the
sun. The mother duck looked on.
Quack, quack, quack!

It was time to go. Slap, slap, slap!

The ducks ran up the hill. ❖

Endings -ed, -ing

Read these words.

swimming	jumped	jumping	waded
taking	hiding	flapped	stepped

Find words that end with **-ed** or **-ing**. Use letters to build words.

j u m p e d

Tell a partner what a duck did. Tell what a frog is doing.

A duck <u>stepped</u> in the pond. A frog is <u>swimming</u> in the pond.

At the Pond

Look at the picture with a partner. Take turns reading the clues. Find the answers in the picture.

1. Find both of the men.
2. Find two kinds of white birds.
3. Find five ducks flying over the pond.
4. Find the bird standing on one leg.
5. Find the frog swimming in the pond.
6. Find rocks piled in the pond.

Acknowledgments

Grateful acknowledgment is given to the authors, artists, photographers, museums, publishers, and agents for permission to reprint copyrighted material. Every effort has been made to secure the appropriate permission. If any omissions have been made or if corrections are required, please contact the Publisher.

Photographic Credits

CVR (Cover) John Giustina/Corbis. **2** (bl) Carlos Alvarez/iStockphoto. (br) Johann Helgason/iStockphoto. (cl) Stephen Aaron Rees/Shutterstock. (cr) jan kranendonk/Shutterstock. (tl) modellocate/Shutterstock. (tr) aida ricciardiello/Shutterstock. **3** (b) Liz Garza Williams/Hampton-Brown/National Geographic School Publishing. (tc) Corbis RF/age fotostock. (tl) DaddyBit/iStockphoto. (tr) Dan Kitwood/Getty Images. **4** Mikhail Palinchak Jr./iStockphoto. **5** Gerry Ellis/Minden Pictures/National Geographic Image Collection. **6** Corbis/SuperStock. **7** Top-Pics TBK/Alamy Images. **8** Dirk Funhoff/Imagebroker RF/age fotostock. **9** A. S. Weaving/Ardea.com. **10** Jason Edwards/National Geographic Image Collection. **11** (t) Liz Garza Williams/Hampton-Brown/National Geographic School Publishing. **12** (b) Angela Hampton Picture Library/Alamy Images. (bc) Distinctive Images/Shutterstock. (t) David Madison/Getty Images. (tc) Rosemarie Gearhart/iStockphoto. **13** (b) Liz Garza Williams/Hampton-Brown/National Geographic School Publishing. (tc) Ian Beames/Ardea.com. (tl) ChrisPole/iStockphoto. (tr) ARCO/J. De Cuveland/age fotostock. **21** (r) Liz Garza Williams/Hampton-Brown/National Geographic School Publishing.

Illustrator Credits

11, 21, 22-23 Jim Paillot; **14-20** Paul Eric Roca

The National Geographic Society

John M. Fahey, Jr., President & Chief Executive Officer
Gilbert M. Grosvenor, Chairman of the Board

National Geographic School Publishing
Hampton-Brown
www.NGSP.com

Printed in the USA.
RR Donnelley, Jefferson City, MO

ISBN:978-0-7362-8035-8

13 14 15 16 17 18 19
10 9 8 7 6 5